To:

From:

*To my biggest supporters of
whatever I do in life,
a.k.a
The Knebel Team!*

This is a work of fiction. All of the names, characters, businesses, places, events and incidents are either the products of the author's imagination or used in a fictitious manner. Any resemblance to actual persons, living or dead, or actual events is purely coincidental.

THE GOLD OF
BLACK ROCK HILL

by C. Knebel
Simple Words Books™

FREE WORKBOOKS
and
FREE ACCESS TO ONLINE SUMMITS

simplewordsbooks.com

Chapter 1

Brisk, The Ship

There are lots of ships at the dock that day. And Brisk is the best ship of all.

Brisk is Big Dan's ship. It was a bandit ship until he got it from a gang of bandits. But Big Dan and his men do not rob things from the rest of the ships. They are not bandits at all. They just hunt for lost gold and ships that sank.

All the ship hands want to get a job on Brisk. Big Dan splits the profits with his men. His men get a shot at getting rich. They all think Big Dan is the best. They want to go on big quests with him. And so does Dex.

Dex is the ship cat on Brisk. His job on the ship is to get rid of the rats. When the ship is not on land, no rats can get on the ship. So he does not have much to do on the trips. He just sits all day on the deck and expects to get his lunch on a dish.

Not much went on at the ship when they were on land. Dex was fed up with sitting still on the ship. He did miss the thrill of the ship rocking up and down.

Dex sits on his cot on the deck as all the ship hands rush to do their jobs. All but Zack and Jeb. They do not do their tasks. They just huff and puff. This is no fun for them.

Zack and Jeb think that Big Dan is a dud. He has a bandit ship. But he

will not be a bandit and rob for fun.
And they cannot stand this.

Dex is not a big fan of Zack and Jeb.
These men like to kick Dex's drink
dish when Big Dan is not there to stop
them.

This is the last day on land for
Brisk. Dex does not get what has kept
Big Dan at land for so long.

In the past, they were in and out of
the dock fast. But not on this visit. Big
Dan went to visit the shops on the dock.
He has told his ship hands that he has
big plans.

If his plans go well, he will get his
hands on an epic thing at the end.

But what can Big Dan's plans be?

He did not tell them that. He kept his big plans to himself. He just told his men to be set to go when he is back on the ship.

Then, he left for the rest of the day.

At last, Brisk is set to go. But Big Dan is not back yet. Dex sits on his cot on the deck with not a thing to do.

It is a hot day. Dex just had a big snack.

"Big Dan will not be back for a bit. What can I do until then?" Dex thinks. "Well, I will not sit on this ship all day. I will visit the dock. I can hunt for a rat." He jumps off his cot. "That will be fun."

Chapter 2

A Cat On The Dock

Dex hops off the ship and trots onto the dock. The dock stinks with all the trash bins from the grill pub.

"There must be big rats on this dock with all this trash," Dex thinks. "It will not be long till a rat pops up."

He sits as still as he can next to a big pig pen on the dock. The pen stinks so bad.

He plans to grab a rat when it runs past. He sits and sits. But there are no rats. Then there is a tap, a scuff and a bump in a trash bin.

"What is that?" Dex gasps.

A rat jumps out of the trash bin. It runs so fast. Dex jumps on the rat but it is a miss.

Then a black cat sprints out of the bin as well. She is small and as thin as a twig.

Quick as a flash, she hops on the rat. She picks it up in her lips.

"That is my rat," Dex yells as he jumps on the small cat.

He bumps into the cat and the cat falls on her back. The rat slips out of her lips and runs off.

"Your rat?" the small cat blasts. "That was not your rat. It was my rat!"

"On your next hunt, I will be glad to help you get a rat," Dex says with zest.

"Oh, and I am Dex by the way."

He is glad to run into a cat on the dock.

"I am Mist," the small cat snaps.

Dex can tell she is not as glad as he is that they met.

"It is fun when rats dash off like that, is it not?" Dex wants to chat.

"It may be fun for you. But that was my lunch," Mist blasts. "I lost my lunch thanks to you! That is no fun at all."

"Oh, do not say that," Dex stops her. "I did not get you to drop it. It is not up to me if you let the rat slip from your lips," he shrugs.

Mist gets upset. "Just go back to where you are from and let me hunt on the dock," she says.

"Well, I had my snack. I was out to hunt a rat for fun," Dex brags. "And I am off back to my ship."

"Oh, a ship cat," Mist sniffs. "You do not hunt for lunch, do you? Is that why you cannot hunt? Just stay on your ship and do not mess things up for me on the dock."

Dex does not like Mist.

He gets up. "Well, I think your dock stinks, and I will not be back to visit you."

"Have a swell day on the ship as I sit with zilch," Mist grunts.

Dex trots off.

Mist spots him getting on to the big ship with a red flag.

"That must be his ship," she thinks. "That cat gets all he wants and just hunts for fun. He has all the luck."

Chapter 3

The Quest

Just as Dex hops on to the ship, Big Dan gets back from his visit to the shops. All his men are glad that Big Dan is back.

"Where were you?" asks Josh.

Josh is the deckman on the ship. He is a kid. So he has to do all the jobs the rest of the men do not want to do. He mops the deck and rubs the rust off the mast.

Big Dan is just to Josh and sticks up for him. He gets Josh hand me down things so Josh does not have to spend his cash.

Dex trusts Josh. He thinks Josh and Big Dan are the best men on the ship.

"Men, I did it!" yells Big Dan. "Check what I got!"

The ship hands rush to check. Big Dan lifts up his hand.

"Is that a map in your hand?" asks Josh.

Big Dan nods. "It is not just a map. It is THE MAP! The map for the Gold of Black Rock Hill!"

"What?" Josh gasps in shock. "But that chest of gold was lost for so long!"

"A lot of men were lost in quests to get their hands on that chest," says a ship hand. "How will we get it when lots of men have not?" he asks.

"Those men did not have this map!" Big Dan says. "That is why they got lost. With this, we will get to that chest!"

"How did you get this map?" asks Josh.

"I got it from an old bandit on land," Big Dan says. "He sells crafts in his gift shop by the docks."

A fat man next to Big Dan says, "A map from a bandit? How can you trust this man?"

"This must be a rip-off," yells a thin man from the back. "If it is not, why did he not dig for the chest himself?"

"I get it," says Big Dan. "But let me tell you why I trust this bandit with all I got. I was just a kid as old as Josh when I met this man. He let me stay with him in his hut. I did not have a thing to pay him with. He did not have much, but he still lent me the cash to get Brisk. He thinks of me as a son."

His men nod.

"I got him help when he was ill," he adds. "He has no kids to pass on the map to. So he let me have it as a gift for helping him. He thinks we can get to it. My gut says we got a shot at this as well."

"So, who will go on a quest with me to get the Gold of Black Rock Hill?" asks Big Dan.

The men lift their fists. They chant and yell. They want to get rich.

"O.K., then!" says Big Dan. "We are on our way!"

Chapter 4

The Flask

The ship hands finish up the last things left.

Big Dan helms the ship out of the dock.

"Off we go!" he yells.

In the wind, the ship drifts from the land. It rocks as it gets on its way.

As men rush to do their jobs, Dex runs up the mast to be out of the way. He spots the ship hands Zack and Jeb hanging back on the deck. They nag that they do not like their jobs. Then Jeb hands a flask to Zack. Zack inspects the flask and sets it in his pocket.

Zack's job is to fix lunch for all the men on the ship. He grills fresh fish on the deck. He picks up the flask from his pocket. He spills drops onto the stack of fish. Then he slips the flask back into his pocket with a grin.

Dex sprints down the mast. Josh runs by the grill with a bucket in his hand.

Zack jumps with a flinch. Dex thinks it is as if Zack does not want Josh to pick up on what he is up to. But the fish smells fantastic. And he forgets all the odd things that just went on.

Zack yells, "Lunch is set. Grab a dish!"

Jeb drops the fish scraps in a bucket. He sets the bucket in the back of the grill. Then he yells, "Fresh fish."

All the men rush to the grill. Zack and Jeb have big grins as they hand out big helpings of fish. All but Zack and Jeb have lots of fish. They skip lunch that day.

As the men have their lunch on the deck, they tell their plans of what they will do with all the gold.

Big Dan sits next to Josh on the bench. He says, "I will fix up my dad's cabin."

An old ship hand says, "I will get a shop at the dock. I just want to be with my grandkids. I do not want to go on trips and quests. If we get the chest, this will be my last."

"What will you get, Josh?" asks Big Dan.

"There is so much stuff I want to get," Josh says with a grin. "But the top thing on my list is to get a crisp set of denim pants. I want to have pants with no rips."

"With that much gold, you can get lots of pants!" Big Dan pats Josh on his back. "Let us finish our lunch. We have a lot to do."

Chapter 5

The Sonnet

"Big Dan, did you check the map yet?" asks Josh.

"I will inspect the map when I finish my lunch." Big Dan hands the map to Josh. "You can check it out, if you like."

Josh flaps the map. There are a lot of things on it.

"This is a big map," Josh says as he inspects it in depth.

"The bandit says most of them are just tricks and traps to get rid of the men who quit fast on this quest," Big Dan says as he sets his dish on the bench.

There is a sonnet on the map. Josh thinks they must crack this sonnet to get to the chest.

You will not get a stack of cash,

Unless you can dig past the ash.

Ash in the chest is just a trick,

To get rich, you just got to stick.

If you have no grit, you must stop,

Your hunt for gold will be a flop.

What you shall have that is a must,

A gang with you that you can trust.

You still may think you are the best,

Yet be quick to get to the chest.

You can get all you want with it,

But the best gift is when it is split.

When you do not fill will with filth,

Ethics is what you end up with.

Josh hands the map back to Big Dan.

Dex slinks up next to the men. He just got fish from a tin can. But he wants Josh or Dan to drop a bit of the fresh fish from the grill for him.

But just then, the fat man says, "Big Dan, I have a twist in my gut."

Josh says, "Oh, I am a bit sick as well."

Big Dan has his hand on his tum. He jumps up. He runs to the back of the ship and vomits.

All the men on the ship get sick. All but Zack and Jeb.

Big Dan tells his men to rest in their beds for the rest of the day. He steps down to his cabin to rest as well. He brings the map with him. But he is so sick that he cannot inspect it.

Zack and Jeb are glad to help the men down the steps to their cabins. Dex thinks this is odd. This is not like Zack and Jeb. They do not like to help the rest.

All the men go to their cabins. It is just Dex left on the deck.

"How did all the ship hands get sick?" he thinks in a panic.

Was the fish bad? Or can it be Zack and Jeb?

Chapter 6

A Visit From Mist

Just then there is a scuff and a sniff from the back of a box.

"Who is there?" Dex asks.

"Hey, Dex," a small black cat says. He is down the steps next to the cabins.

It is Mist from the dock.

"It is you! Why are you on my ship?" Dex asks. "How did you get on the ship?"

Mist jumps onto the deck. She blinks in the sun.

"I do not want to hunt for my lunch." She licks her lips. "I want to be a ship cat just as you are. So, I got on this ship, the big ship with the red flag. But I am wet. And I get sick when the ship rocks. This is not much fun."

"You cannot just jump on a ship and be a ship cat, Mist," Dex says. "There is so much to the job."

Mist is sad. "I want to be back on my dock. But I am stuck on this ship!"

"Just rest a bit. It will not be long until we are back on land. I cannot get you off until then," Dex says.

Mist nods. "Well, I smell fish!"

She steps in front of a dish a man had left on the deck from lunch. "Can I get a bit of this for lunch?"

"No!" Dex kicks the dish out of the way.

Mist stops when Dex yells.

"That fish got the men sick. I think it will be bad for a cat as well. Things are getting odd on this ship," he adds.

Just then, steps thud up to the deck.

Dex says, "Hush!"

He and Mist duck into a box at the back of a skiff.

Jeb and Zack step onto the deck. "Ha ha!" says Zack. "That was fun. We got all the men sick on the ship. They are out of our way."

"Yes," Jeb grins. "This is the best plan! And it is still on!"

"We got Big Dan sick. We can slink into his cabin when the sun is down and grab the map," Zack says.

Jeb rubs his hands. "If we get the map, then we get the gold! And we will be rich."

Then Zack stops and says, "But Jeb, there is a thing we did not think of."

"What is that?" Jeb asks.

"Well," Zack says. "If we rob the map, Big Dan will tell it is missing. Then he will suspect what we are up to."

Jeb grunts. "Hmm, that will be bad."

He thinks for a bit. Then he says, "What if we do not get the map, but just shift where the X is on the map? We send them to dig in a spot with no gold. Then we can dig and get the gold!"

"Fantastic plan!" Zack says. "Let us do it when Big Dan naps," he adds. "The bad stuff in the fish will not last long. We must fix the map quick!"

Chapter 7

The X On The Map

"Oh, no!" Dex says. "They want to rob the gold! We must stop them."

Mist grunts. "We? There is no we. This is not my ship. You stop them if you must."

"But those are bad men!" Dex begs.

Mist shrugs. "I do not want to be in this mess. I just want to get off this ship. Plus, I am sick. I just cannot help."

Dex gets upset with Mist. Jeb and Zack have a plot to rob the gold! And yet, this selfish cat says she will not help.

Zack and Jeb hang out on the deck until the sun sets. Then they go down to Big Dan's cabin.

Dex slinks out of the box. A panic kicks in. He cannot think of what to do to stop the bad men. He sprints to Big Dan's cabin.

Jeb and Zack are in there, hunting for the map. Big Dan is still in his bed. He has no hint who is in the cabin. Dex slips in. Jeb and Zack do not spot him.

"Where is this map?" Zack asks.

He lifts the lid of the lockbox on Big Dan's desk. The map is not in it.

Jeb checks the shelf. But there is still no map.

"We must be quick, or he will get up!" Jeb says.

As the men hunt with no luck, Dex thinks, "I wish Big Dan just got up. Then they cannot get their hands on the map!"

But just then, Zack spots Big Dan's pants.

"The pocket!" he says. "The map was in his pocket!"

He picks up the pants and checks Big Dan's pockets.

"Is that it?" Jeb asks.

"Yes," Zack says with a grin. "We got the map for the chest."

Jeb asks, "Where is the chest?"

"At the X," Zack taps on the map. "The X is on the top of a hill next to a big black rock." Then he grins. "But not for long!"

"Ha ha!" yells Jeb.

"Hush!" says Zack.

He sets the map on the desk. He scans it.

Then, he rubs out the X. But he cannot get rid of it.

"Can you just cut out the X from the map?" Jeb grunts.

"Cut the map!" Zack smacks Jeb. "I do not think so!"

Zack gets a scrap and drafts the map on it.

He jots down where the chest is onto his pad. He drops black ink on the map. The ink masks the X. Then, he adds a big fresh X next to a pond a long way off from the hill.

"Let us get out quick!" Jeb tells Zack.

Zack sets the map back in Big Dan's pocket. The men dash out of the cabin.

"This is a mess," thinks Dex. "I must tell all this to Big Dan."

But how?

Chapter 8

Selfish Mist

Dex sits by Big Dan's bed until the next day. Big Dan gets up when Josh runs into his cabin in a rush.

"Josh!" Big Dan says. "Are you O.K.? How are the rest of the men?"

"We are all well. It was a big help to rest. And check this out, Big Dan!" Josh has a small black cat in his hands.

Dex grunts as he spots Mist.

"Where did you get that cat?" asks Big Dan.

"She was in a box on the deck," Josh says as he rubs the cat's back.

"It will be fun for Dex to have a pal on the ship," says Big Dan.

Dex does not like this a bit. The last thing he wants is to hang out with Mist.

Big Dan and Josh step up onto the deck. Dex runs up as well. Josh brings Mist with him.

Mist jumps down on the deck. Jeb spots the small cat.

"A black cat on the ship? Is that not bad luck?" he gasps.

"Not at all." Big Dan bends down and pats Mist's back.

"I do not like black cats," Jeb grunts.

Josh brings Mist snacks and milk in a small pot. Then, he lets Mist nap on Dex's cot.

Josh can tell that Dex is upset at all this fuss.

"Let her have your cot, Dex," Josh tells him. "She is thin and small. I will split your snacks with her as well."

"She is a selfish cat," Dex thinks. "She will get the snacks from Josh, but she will not help Dex stop the bad men who want to rob the gold."

All the men are on the deck. They do their jobs and discuss how bad that fish was.

Jeb and Zack act as if they got sick as well.

"It must be that fish we had for lunch," says Zack. "I am sad that Jeb and I got all of you sick with that bad fish."

Big Dan pats Zack on the back.

"Do not be sad," he says. "It was just a small slip up."

Zack winks at Jeb.

Dex is upset that he still has no plan on how to tell Big Dan that the map is a sham.

"Where will the map bring the men to?" Dex thinks.

Not to the chest of gold.

As Jeb and Zack go past, Dex lets out a big hiss.

Mist jumps off the cot and steps up to Dex.

"Why did you hiss at them?" she asks.

"They are the men who want to rob the chest," he says. "They have a big plot. I wish you had a bit of a plan to help."

Mist shrugs. "The map and the chest of gold do not benefit me."

"Is this how you say thanks?" asks Dex.

Mist blasts. "I have to stick up for me on the docks with no help. I have to fend for myself to get what I can when I can. When we get to land, I will be off this ship."

Then she trots to Josh. He has got a dish of milk for the cats. Mist sips her milk in no stress.

Dex can tell that Mist will be no help at all.

Chapter 9

The Land

All the men stop and run to the front of the deck when the man on the mast yells, "Land! Land! Land!"

"There it is!" Josh yells. "The chest must be on that land!"

Big Dan is at the helm. He taps the map in his pocket.

"This will be a grand day!" he says to his men. "We will dig out the chest. We will all be rich!"

All men on the deck clap and yell.

Big Dan tells his men to bring down a skiff. Then he adds, "It is a hot day.

Do not forget to pack up drinks."

Josh is sad that he cannot go on the land with the rest to dig for the gold. Big Dan tells him that a ship hand must stay back on the ship. And Josh gets the jobs that no man wants to do. So it will be he who is left on the ship.

Zack and Jeb do not want to go on the land with Big Dan and his men. They have a plot that will let them stay on the ship just for a bit until the men are out of their way.

Zack brings out the bucket with the fish scraps he hid in the back of the grill. He sets the bucket on the top of the steps. Then he kicks it down. But he acts as if he trips on the bucket.

Thump, thump, bang, crash!

The bucket tips and bumps down the steps. It lands next to Josh. All the fish bits spill on the steps and the deck.

This all fits in with their big scam.

Josh grunts. "Who left this trash up the steps?"

Zack runs down the steps.

"Who did that mess?" asks Big Dan.

Zack jumps in, "It was this kid. He must have left a bucket of fish on the steps."

Josh does not get to say a thing.

Jeb nods. "This is the fish that got us all sick. We cannot let it just be on the deck. It will stink up the ship!"

"And what if the cats snack on it? They will be sick as well," adds Zack. "Let us get rid of this quick. Jeb and I will stay on the ship and help Josh scrub the fish off the deck. But you must go off and get the gold."

Jeb and Zack grab mops as Dan and the men go off on the skiffs. But they do not intend to help Josh at all.

"O.K." Big Dan nods. "Thank you for helping Josh scrub the deck."

Then he adds, "Josh, fix eggs and ham for the cats when you get rid of this big mess."

"I am on it, Big Dan," Josh says. But he still wants to be in the quest on land.

Big Dan pats his pocket to check the map is still there. Then he and his men jump on a skiff.

It is just Zack, Jeb and Josh left on the ship. And the cats.

Zack and Jeb grin. Their plan is on track.

The skiff brings Big Dan and his men to the land. They stand on the sand as Big Dan gets the map from his pocket.

He checks which way to go. He thinks this is the valid map. Yet, what he has in his hand will not bring them to the chest.

He twists the map left and inspects it. Then he lifts his hand to the left.

"We go this way!" he tells his men. "The X on the map brings us to the west. We pass the shrubs and get to the pond. Then we will dig for the chest next to the big red rock."

Big Dan thinks it is a bit odd that the Gold of Black Rock Hill is not on a hill, but it is by a pond. Plus, the rock is red, not black.

But that is what is on the map. He sticks with what the map says.

They go on the path by the shrubs.

Chapter 10

Josh Sniffs A Scam

Back on the ship, Mist is finishing a big dish of eggs. She licks her chops and sits on the deck.

Dex is still upset with her.

"Of all the cats I have met, you are the most selfish," he says.

"I am just a small cat. What can I do?" asks Mist. "I cannot help them. That is for you as well."

"If we sit back, we will be of no help. But there must be a way. We just may get a bit of luck and fix this," Dex says.

What Dex says gets Mist to think.

Jeb and Zack drop their mops when the skiff has left. They hang out by the helm.

"Do not miss that spot there," Jeb yells at Josh with a grin, as Josh scrubs the mess on the deck.

"We will go to land as well. It is best if we help the rest to dig for the chest," Zack tells Josh. "You can just finish up on the deck."

As they bring down a skiff, Dex spots a scrap fall onto the deck from Zack's pocket. The men jump on the skiff and off they go.

Dex picks the scrap up and checks it out.

"Yes!" he jumps up with a thrill.

"What is that?" Mist asks.

"It is the draft of the valid map!" Dex says. "This tells us where the chest is. If we can get it to Big Dan, Zack and Jeb's plot will end!"

"I want to help," she says to Dex. "If you let me."

Dex nods.

He steps in front of Josh with the draft in his lips. Mist runs up to Josh as well.

Josh grunts as he mops. He does not stop to check on Dex and Mist.

Next, Dex runs laps on the deck.

Mist hops up and down. Josh grins.

He thinks the cats are having fun.

The cats bug Josh. But he still does not stop mopping the deck. They tug his pants until he drops his mop.

Josh bends and pats the cats.

"I still have so much to do," he says. "I cannot stop to play with you."

Dex drops the draft in front of him as Josh picks up his mop.

"What is that, Dex?" Josh asks.

He picks up the scrap and scans it.

"This is a draft of the map to the chest!" he gasps. "What Big Dan had when we had lunch was a big map, not this draft. Who had this? Where did you get this from?"

Mist runs to the mops Zack and Jeb had. She jumps on them.

Josh thinks fast. "Zack and Jeb!" he yells.

"Yes!" nod Dex and Mist.

"I did not trust those men a bit! Big Dan is not on the track to the chest, is he?" Josh lifts down the last skiff. He jumps on it fast. Mist and Dex jump in the skiff as well. And they are off to the land.

Chapter 11

Tracks On The Sand

When Josh and the cats are on land, they jump off the skiff and onto the sand. Josh has the draft of the map with him.

They want to tell all this to Big Dan. So he can track down Zack and Jeb and get to the chest.

But Josh cannot tell which way Big Dan and his men went.

Dex yelps when he spots a thing in the sand. Josh and Mist run to Dex. There is a track with prints.

"This must be the path Big Dan and his men went on," Josh says.

They run off on the path fast. But they miss the track next to it with lots of prints.

They sprint on the path until the sand ends. Then they stop when there are no prints left.

Mist and Dex sniff the grass. Then run a bit. Then they stop to sniff.

Josh treks with the cats. He trusts that they got this. They end up by a hill. Then there is yelling.

Josh gasps. This is not Big Dan and the ship hands. It is Jeb and Zack!

Jeb and Zack stand with their backs to the path. They do not spot Josh and the cats.

"Where is our map?" Zack yells at Jeb.

"I do not have it. You had it in your pocket," Jeb yells back. "Did you drop it?"

"I do not drop things that will get me rich!" Zack snaps. "Check your pockets."

Jeb pats his pants.

"It is not on me," he says. "If we are fast, we can dash back to the ship to check if you left it there. Then we can get back. Big Dan and the rest will still be digging at the spot we sent them to."

Josh tells the cats, "Let us go back. I do not want them to spot us."

But he steps on a branch and it cracks with a big snap.

Chapter 12

Dig For The Gold

Jeb and Zack flinch when they spot Josh and the cats.

"Grab that kid quick!" yells Jeb. "He must have got what I just told you!"

Josh runs, but he trips. Zack grabs the kid. Dex sinks his fangs into Zack's leg to stop him.

"Get this cat off me!" Zack yelps. He still has Josh in his grip.

Jeb grabs Dex by the scruff of his neck and lifts up the cat. Dex twists and flings his legs, but he cannot get down.

"Quick, Mist!" Dex says. "It is up to you! Go and get Big Dan!"

Mist is off, quick as a shot. She runs and runs.

Jeb stuffs Dex into a sack.

Zack spots the map in Josh's pocket as he straps Josh's hands to his back.

"Well, well, well. Check what Josh has in his pocket," Zack mocks Josh. "I am glad that you bring the map back to us," he grins.

"The plan is back on track," Jeb says.

With the map, Zack and Jeb can tell which way the chest is.

They go to the top of the hill. At the top, there is a black rock just as the map says.

"This is it!" Jeb says. "This is where the map brings us... to the Gold of Black Rock Hill!"

Josh sits on a log, his hands still held with straps. Dex picks at the sack with his fangs. But he cannot get out.

The men dig for a bit.

Jeb grunts. "It is hot. I want to rest."

"Just stick with the plan. Do you want that gold or not?" blasts Zack.

"I will stop for a bit," Jeb insists. He grabs his jug. "I must have a drink."

He gets a sip.

Then he says, "Zack, we got Dex. But that black cat ran off."

"She cannot do a thing," Zack says. "Cats cannot get what we say. And if she does, how can she tell Big Dan what we are up to?"

"I tell you she is bad luck," Jeb hums.

The men get back to digging as fast as they can. There is a thud as Jeb hits a mass.

"It is the chest! We got it!" the bad men yell.

Chapter 13

Mist's Big Run

Mist sprints down the hill and all the way back to the sand. She runs so fast, she thinks her legs will just quit. But they do not.

"I cannot stop. I will not stop," she pants.

Then she spots the next track with the prints in the sand.

"There are lots of prints on this track. This must be the path to Big Dan," Mist thinks.

She gets to a bunch of shrubs. Her legs are limp. She is spent. But she picks herself up.

"Press on, Mist!" she tells herself. "This will get me to Big Dan."

And off she runs.

When she is by the pond, there is chatting. At last! It is Big Dan and his men.

There are lots of pits where they have dug all day. But they have not hit gold.

"This is a bust!" says the fat man. "There is no chest."

"No, men, we have to go on digging," Big Dan says. "I do not want to quit just yet."

Just then a ship hand spots Mist. "Is that the black cat that was on the ship?" he asks.

Big Dan stops to dig, "Yes. How did she get off the ship?"

Mist cannot think how to tell Big Dan that he must go with her.

"You must help!" she wants to yell. "Dex is stuck in a sack. Zack and Jeb got Josh. And they are digging for your chest!"

She runs off a bit. Then she runs back to him and tugs his pants' leg.

But Big Dan and the men do not get what Mist wants to tell them.

"Is that cat sick?" asks a ship hand.

"I do not think so," Big Dan taps his chin. "How did she get onto land? She was not on the skiff with us. And cats cannot swim that long."

Mist runs off and gets back, but Big Dan still does not get it.

Then she spots the map in front of Big Dan. She springs up and grabs it, then sprints off with it.

"Stop that cat!" yells Big Dan. "Track her down. She has our map!"

"At last!" Mist thinks, as she runs off with the map and the men run in the back.

Chapter 14

The Chest Of Ash

With a big thrill, Jeb and Zack dig up the chest. They yank it out of the pit.

"We will be so rich!" Jeb rubs his hands.

"You will not get off with all the gold," Josh yells. "Big Dan will bring you down."

"Shut up, kid," snaps Zack. "Big Dan is stuck next to a bunch of shrubs by the pond. They are digging for zilch!"

Jeb hits the lock on the chest with a big rock. The lock falls off.

He yanks off the lid of the chest to check out the gold.

But there is no gold. Just a big pack of ash in the chest.

"What is this?" Jeb yells.

Zack says, "The ash may be just on the top. Dig in."

Jeb stuffs his hands in and digs out lumps of ash. "Where is the gold?"

The men tip the chest. The stash of ash spills out. But there is no gold.

The men yell and kick the chest. They smash it to bits.

"Where is my gold?" Zack yells.

"Where is OUR gold?" Jeb yells back.

Josh thinks of the map that Big Dan had at lunch. It had a sonnet on it.

He thinks of what the sonnet says:

"You will not get a stack of cash,

Unless you can dig past the ash.

Ash in the chest is just a trick,

To get rich you just got to stick..."

He cannot think how the sonnet ends. But this bit may just have all the hints to get to the gold.

In a flash, he gets it. He can tell where the chest with the gold is. But he will not tell them. Not at all.

Zack says, "We got to go back to the ship. And we have to get rid of this kid. He will tell Big Dan what we did."

"How do we do that?" Jeb asks.

Zack thinks for a bit.

"The skiff," he says. "We drill into it. Then we send the skiff out with the kid in it. We can tell Big Dan that Josh went to be with them and the skiff sank on its way to the land. Then he will not think it was us."

"I like that!" says Jeb. "Let us get the cat in the skiff when we are at it. I just do not like this cat."

Zack nods.

"No!" yells Josh. "Let the cat go! He cannot tell a thing!"

Jeb grabs Josh. Zack picks up the sack. They drag them down on the path back to the sand.

"Stop it! Let us go!" Josh yells.

Jeb sits Josh in the skiff. He sets a gag on Josh, so Josh cannot call for help.

Zack casts the sack next to Josh. Dex is still in it.

Quick as a flash, the men drill into the skiff. They tug it off the land. The sack gets wet as the skiff fills. Dex still tugs at the sack with his fangs. But no luck. He is stuck in the sack.

Josh thinks the skiff will sink with them in it. He thinks this is the end. But he still tells Dex, "Do not panic! We will get out of this mess."

Chapter 15

The Big Scam Flops

Mist runs out of the shrubs. She drops on the sand by the skiffs just next to Jeb and Zack.

But where are Josh and Dex? She cannot spot them.

Big Dan and his men run up to the skiffs. They spot Jeb and Zack. Jeb has a drill in his hand.

"What is up with you?" Big Dan asks. "What is that in your hand? Is that a drill?"

Jeb says, "We got to land to check how the gold hunt went. Did you get the gold yet?"

Big Dan is sad.

"No, it was a flop. We did our best, but there was no chest of gold." He spots the skiff. "Is that a skiff out there?"

"What skiff?" Jeb shrugs.

"There it is!" Big Dan yells in shock. "Is that Josh in it?"

A ship hand yells, "That skiff is sinking!"

"What?" Big Dan gasps. "Men! Help!"

Big Dan and a ship man jump in and swim to the skiff fast. Josh is in the skiff with his hands at his back. Dex is still in the sack.

Big Dan cuts the band on Josh's hand and gets the gag off. He gets Josh out of the skiff. He helps him swim back.

The ship hand grabs the skiff and yanks it to land. He gets Dex out of the sack. Dex is all wet, but he is O.K.

Josh hugs Big Dan. Then he falls down on the sand next to Mist.

Big Dan asks, "Who did this to you, Josh?"

Josh pants, "It was them! Zack and Jeb! They got you a sham map and they had a plot to get all the gold!"

Zack yells at Big Dan, "We did not do such a thing. You cannot trust this kid."

Big Dan is upset. "Men! Grab these scums!"

The ship hands grab Zack and Jeb as they kick and yell.

Then Jeb scoffs, "Well, you got us. But you will not get a sniff of gold. It was just a big box of ash!"

"No," Josh says. "That was just a test! And you did not pass it. Check the valid map, not the scam."

Big Dan grabs the valid map.

Josh adds, "Zack and Jeb hid the X by the hills with the ink. Then they set a scam X next to the red rock by the pond. But the sonnet tells it all if you stop and think."

Big Dan checks the map.

"You will not get a stack of cash,

Unless you can dig past the ash.

Ash in the chest is a trick,

To get rich you just got to stick..."

Josh says, "Jeb and Zack dug out the chest with ash. But if you go on digging, you will get to the chest with the gold!"

"Tell us where to go!" says Big Dan.

He and a bunch of men sprint off with Josh.

Chapter 16

Rich As A King

Mist and Dex sit on the sand.

Dex says, "For such a selfish cat, you did well."

Mist grins. "I am a bit sick of that selfish cat thing. I like to have pals who have my back."

In a bit, the men and Josh are back with a big chest.

"Gold! Gold! We got the chest of gold! We will be as rich as a king!"

Zack and Jeb are glum as the ship hands lug the big chest on the skiff.

This is a lot of gold!

When Brisk gets back to the dock, Big Dan hands Jeb and Zack to the cops.

Big Dan splits the gold with his men. They all get rich.

Big Dan thinks that all his men will quit now that they have all that cash to spend. But the men want to stay on Brisk and go on the next quest with Big Dan. Just the old ship hand calls it a day. He will get his shop by the dock and spend his days with his grandkids.

Dex is glad for all this.

He asks Mist, "Will you go back to the dock and hunt rats for lunch?"

Mist says, "No, I am sick of that. I do not miss it at all."

"Well," Dex says, "I think we have a spot for a small ship cat on Brisk. Do you want the job?"

Mist grins.

"Well, if you insist."

You can download full color

CERTIFICATE OF ACCOMPLISHMENT
and
CERTIFICATE OF COMPLETION

On our website

SIMPLEWORDSBOOKS.COM

Certificate of Accomplishment

This certificate is awarded to

_____

for successful completion of

The Gold of Black Rock Hill

_____   _____
Signature   Date

SIMPLE WORDS

THE GOLD OF
BLACK ROCK HILL
WORD LIST

#	Word	Count	#	Word	Count	#	Word	Count
1	a	197	26	bends	2	51	cabin	8
2	act	1	27	benefit	1	52	cabins	3
3	acts	1	28	best	8	53	call	1
4	adds	8	29	big	141	54	calls	1
5	all	56	30	bin	3	55	can	36
6	am	13	31	bins	1	56	cannot	26
7	an	3	32	bit	20	57	cash	6
8	and	167	33	bits	2	58	casts	1
9	are	41	34	black	15	59	cat	34
10	as	61	35	blasts	4	60	cats	16
11	ash	12	36	blinks	1	61	chant	1
12	asks	26	37	box	5	62	chat	1
13	at	33	38	brags	1	63	chatting	1
14	back	49	39	branch	1	64	check	13
15	backs	1	40	bring	6	65	checks	5
16	bad	13	41	brings	7	66	chest	42
17	band	1	42	Brisk	10	67	chin	1
18	bandit	7	43	bucket	8	68	chops	1
19	bandits	2	44	bug	1	69	clap	1
20	bang	1	45	bump	1	70	cops	1
21	be	48	46	bumps	2	71	cot	6
22	bed	2	47	bunch	3	72	crack	1
23	beds	1	48	bust	1	73	cracks	1
24	begs	1	49	but	64	74	crafts	1
25	bench	2	50	by	15	75	crash	1

#	Word	Count
76	crisp	1
77	cut	2
78	cuts	1
79	dad	1
80	Dan	114
81	dash	3
82	day	14
83	days	1
84	deck	29
85	deckman	1
86	denim	1
87	depth	1
88	desk	2
89	Dex	98
90	did	28
91	dig	14
92	digging	6
93	digs	1
94	discuss	1
95	dish	8
96	do	56
97	dock	19
98	docks	2
99	does	12
100	down	25

#	Word	Count
101	draft	6
102	drafts	1
103	drag	1
104	drifts	1
105	drill	4
106	drink	2
107	drinks	1
108	drop	5
109	drops	6
110	duck	1
111	dud	1
112	dug	2
113	eggs	2
114	end	5
115	ends	2
116	epic	1
117	ethics	1
118	expects	1
119	fall	1
120	falls	3
121	fan	1
122	fangs	3
123	fantastic	2
124	fast	10
125	fat	3

#	Word	Count
126	fed	1
127	fend	1
128	fill	1
129	fills	1
130	filth	1
131	finish	4
132	finishing	1
133	fish	21
134	fists	1
135	fits	1
136	fix	5
137	flag	2
138	flaps	1
139	flash	3
140	flask	4
141	flinch	2
142	flings	1
143	flop	2
144	for	51
145	forget	1
146	forgets	1
147	fresh	4
148	from	22
149	front	5
150	fun	12

#	Word	Count		#	Word	Count		#	Word	Count
151	fuss	1		176	gut	2		201	him	18
152	gag	2		177	ha	4		202	himself	2
153	gang	2		178	had	13		203	hint	1
154	gasps	6		179	ham	1		204	hints	1
155	get	86		180	hand	19		205	his	80
156	gets	21		181	hands	24		206	hiss	2
157	getting	3		182	hang	3		207	hit	1
158	gift	3		183	hanging	1		208	hits	2
159	glad	7		184	has	19		209	hmm	1
160	glum	1		185	have	38		210	hops	4
161	go	32		186	having	1		211	hot	3
162	gold	41		187	he	172		212	how	17
163	got	31		188	held	1		213	huff	1
164	grab	7		189	helm	2		214	hugs	1
165	grabs	7		190	helms	1		215	hums	1
166	grand	1		191	help	20		216	hunt	12
167	grandkids	2		192	helping	2		217	hunting	1
168	grass	1		193	helpings	1		218	hunts	1
169	grill	6		194	helps	1		219	hush	2
170	grills	1		195	her	14		220	hut	1
171	grin	5		196	herself	2		221	I	93
172	grins	7		197	hey	1		222	if	24
173	grip	1		198	hid	2		223	ill	1
174	grit	1		199	hill	10		224	in	76
175	grunts	9		200	hills	1		225	ink	3

#	Word	Count
226	insist	1
227	insists	1
228	inspect	2
229	inspects	3
230	intend	1
231	into	10
232	is	170
233	it	111
234	its	2
235	Jeb	87
236	job	5
237	jobs	6
238	Josh	103
239	jots	1
240	jug	1
241	jump	6
242	jumps	13
243	just	55
244	kept	2
245	kick	3
246	kicks	3
247	kid	9
248	kids	1
249	king	1
250	land	24

#	Word	Count
251	lands	1
252	laps	1
253	last	9
254	left	13
255	leg	2
256	legs	3
257	lent	1
258	let	17
259	lets	2
260	licks	2
261	lid	2
262	lift	1
263	lifts	5
264	like	12
265	limp	1
266	lips	5
267	list	1
268	lock	2
269	lockbox	1
270	log	1
271	long	8
272	lost	5
273	lot	4
274	lots	7
275	luck	6

#	Word	Count
276	lug	1
277	lumps	1
278	lunch	17
279	man	10
280	map	65
281	masks	1
282	mass	1
283	mast	4
284	may	5
285	me	17
286	men	67
287	mess	7
288	met	3
289	milk	3
290	miss	5
291	missing	1
292	Mist	58
293	mocks	1
294	mop	2
295	mopping	1
296	mops	5
297	most	2
298	much	8
299	must	23
300	my	19

#	Word	Count	#	Word	Count	#	Word	Count
301	myself	1	326	pals	1	351	prints	5
302	nag	1	327	panic	3	352	profits	1
303	nap	1	328	pants	10	353	pub	1
304	naps	1	329	pass	3	354	puff	1
305	neck	1	330	past	6	355	quest	4
306	next	20	331	path	7	356	quests	3
307	no	31	332	pats	6	357	quick	10
308	nod	2	333	pay	1	358	quit	4
309	nods	6	334	pen	2	359	ran	1
310	not	105	335	pick	1	360	rat	14
311	now	1	336	picks	9	361	rats	6
312	O.K.	4	337	pig	1	362	red	5
313	odd	4	338	pit	1	363	rest	14
314	of	102	339	pits	1	364	rich	11
315	off	35	340	plan	7	365	rid	6
316	oh	5	341	plans	6	366	rip-off	1
317	old	4	342	play	1	367	rips	1
318	on	154	343	plot	5	368	rob	7
319	onto	9	344	plus	2	369	rock	10
320	or	4	345	pocket	13	370	rocking	1
321	our	7	346	pockets	2	371	rocks	2
322	out	37	347	pond	6	372	rubs	5
323	pack	2	348	pops	1	373	run	7
324	pad	1	349	pot	1	374	runs	22
325	pal	1	350	press	1	375	rush	5

#	Word	Count	#	Word	Count	#	Word	Count
376	rust	1	401	she	47	426	slinks	2
377	sack	10	402	shelf	1	427	slip	2
378	sad	5	403	shift	1	428	slips	3
379	sand	10	404	ship	75	429	smacks	1
380	sank	2	405	ships	3	430	small	12
381	say	4	406	shock	2	431	smash	1
382	says	70	407	shop	3	432	smell	1
383	scam	3	408	shops	2	433	smells	1
384	scans	2	409	shot	3	434	snack	3
385	scoffs	1	410	shrubs	5	435	snacks	3
386	scrap	4	411	shrugs	4	436	snap	1
387	scraps	2	412	shut	1	437	snaps	3
388	scrub	2	413	sick	16	438	sniff	4
389	scrubs	1	414	sink	1	439	sniffs	1
390	scruff	1	415	sinking	1	440	so	22
391	scuff	2	416	sinks	1	441	son	1
392	scums	1	417	sip	1	442	sonnet	6
393	selfish	5	418	sips	1	443	spend	3
394	sells	1	419	sit	4	444	spent	1
395	send	2	420	sits	11	445	spill	1
396	sent	1	421	sitting	1	446	spills	2
397	set	5	422	skiff	28	447	split	2
398	sets	8	423	skiffs	3	448	splits	2
399	shall	1	424	skip	1	449	spot	10
400	sham	2	425	slink	1	450	spots	12

#	Word	Count
451	springs	1
452	sprint	2
453	sprints	5
454	stack	4
455	stand	3
456	stash	1
457	stay	6
458	step	2
459	steps	14
460	stick	5
461	sticks	2
462	still	21
463	stink	1
464	stinks	3
465	stop	19
466	stops	4
467	straps	2
468	stress	1
469	stuck	4
470	stuff	2
471	stuffs	2
472	such	2
473	sun	3
474	suspect	1
475	swell	1

#	Word	Count
476	swim	3
477	tap	1
478	taps	3
479	tasks	1
480	tell	22
481	tells	12
482	test	1
483	thank	1
484	thanks	2
485	that	85
486	the	513
487	their	18
488	them	21
489	then	47
490	there	34
491	these	2
492	they	68
493	thin	3
494	thing	12
495	things	8
496	think	15
497	thinks	28
498	this	75
499	those	3
500	thrill	3

#	Word	Count
501	thud	2
502	thump	2
503	till	1
504	tin	1
505	tip	1
506	tips	1
507	to	209
508	told	3
509	top	6
510	track	9
511	traps	1
512	trash	5
513	treks	1
514	trick	3
515	tricks	1
516	trips	4
517	trots	3
518	trust	5
519	trusts	2
520	tug	2
521	tugs	2
522	tum	1
523	twig	1
524	twist	1
525	twists	2

#	Word	Count
526	unless	3
527	until	9
528	up	50
529	upset	6
530	us	17
531	valid	4
532	visit	5
533	vomits	1
534	want	27
535	wants	8
536	was	26
537	way	15
538	we	68
539	well	27
540	went	7
541	were	4
542	west	1
543	wet	3
544	what	37
545	when	30
546	where	19
547	which	3
548	who	12
549	why	6
550	will	72

#	Word	Count
551	wind	1
552	winks	1
553	wish	2
554	with	80
555	X	10
556	yank	1
557	yanks	2
558	yell	6
559	yelling	1
560	yells	25
561	yelps	2
562	yes	5
563	yet	7
564	you	89
565	your	14
566	Zack	88
567	zest	1
568	zilch	2
Total Words		**7387**

Do you want to write your own story now?

Written by:
_____

_____

_____

_____

_____

_____

_____

_____

_____

_____

_____

_____

_____

_____

_____

_____

_____

_____

_____

_____

_____

_____

Do you want to draw your own story now?

Illustrated by:

WANT TO READ
MORE
CHAPTER BOOKS

STUDY GUIDES
AND
HANDBOOKS

www.simplewordsbooks.com

VISIT OUR WEBSITE FOR FREE RESOURCES

simplewordsbooks.com

AND CHECK OUT OUR FREE ONLINE SUMMITS

Made in the USA
Columbia, SC
12 September 2020